dear Brent:
So go[...]
you he[...]
Barnes & [...]
11.18.16
New Brunswick

EMPIRE WASTED

Becca Klaver

Empire Wasted
© 2016 Becca Klaver
20 19 18 17 16   1 2 3 4 5
First Edition

Design & composition: Shanna Compton, shannacompton.com
Cover photo: Daniel Arnold, www.daniel-arnold.org

Published by Bloof Books
www.bloofbooks.com
New Jersey

Bloof Books are printed in the USA by Bookmobile and Spencer Printing. Booksellers, libraries, and other institutions may order direct from us by contacting sales@bloofbooks.com. POD copies are distributed via Ingram, Baker & Taylor, and other wholesalers. Individuals may purchase our books direct from our website, from online retailers such as Amazon.com, or request them from their favorite bookstores.

Please support your local independent bookseller whenever possible.

ISBN-13: 978-0-9965868-4-9
ISBN-10: 0-9965868-4-9

1. American poetry—21st century. 2. Poets, American—21st century.

∞ This paper meets the requirements of ANSI/NISO Z39.48-1992

Contents

To gaze into this darkness of the present—this light that tries to reach us but cannot—this is what it means to be contemporary.

—Anne Waldman, *The Brooklyn Rail* (2016)

Hold back the edges of your gowns, Ladies, we are going through hell.

—William Carlos Williams, introduction to *Howl and Other Poems* (1956)

Death & Disaster Series

"Everything's Been Recruited"

To learn which side you're on
you pick someone to follow
through the city streets
then see how far you'll go.
If you enter the foyer, oy vey,
then you are on our side.
If you go into the boudoir,
that far, you are on the side
of the enemy. If you board
the plane, you might find
yourself a red name on a
black list. If you feel only
a terror of the domestic
but not a *terroir* foreign,
they have a remedy for that,
but it can only be prescribed
if you were wed in a way
their instruments can detect
and if you have never suffered
from a similar terror before.
They administrate analogy but
we only want you to show us,
through a stashpile of choices
and the small acts you perform
each day, which side you are on.
Till the earth. Kill the earth.
Swallow scoops of wet dirt.
Which side are you on?

Super Tuesday

We soaped up and shaved off your beard, gave into playing the leaked album set for spring release.

I asked *How you do* and you were a border skirmish or a sinkhole.

You asked *How did you sleep* but there were glyphs I couldn't read in my dreams again. So the answer was shitty. The answer was typical.

The cat was starting to shed. What did her fur know that we didn't? If I left the door open, how far would she go? And you

had stolen over to the polling place to string lights along the gutters. Crouched on the roof, hounding dawn, tongue stuck to the lightning rod.

Red Arrow Down

Quarterlife bodies tap toes
picture foreign airports at Christmas
imagine Japanese characters for

connecting flight

tattooed on our tailbones

bitchy reveries
evolutionary tailspins
dream the dream of averages

    sticky bar stool on the eastside
    hatchback for weekend errands

      We are falling off

The more we get to know you
      the more
the overlong petticoat of pettiness scratches our ankles
      nips at our heels
            sinks in, fangy

After the crash
      everyone laughs

at our lunchtime propositions
and begs instead for travelogues

Choose-your-own-imagination-replacement

NO VACANCY

IMPLIES A FULLNESS

sputters neon in passing

"Under the terrible burden of destiny laughing as a young man laughs"

Will the mannequins come to life
Will the sky crack and drip yolk
Will the machinery catch on itself
Will the bloody kerchief read *mandate*
Will the circle be unbroken
Will the manatees burst through the glass
Will the cement shake and shriek
Will Sue clamber anciently toward the green
Will the darkness drop again
Will somebody please help us
Will the shadows of desert birds reel
Will the skyline stand
Will Studs be a benevolent god
Will the experiment work

[November 4, 2008]

"We Got Him"

NBC News interrupts The Celebrity Apprentice *to inform viewers that President Obama will be delivering an important statement from the White House*

•

Don't believe Osama Bin Laden was a real thing in the first place duh

Can this week get any more surreal? Seriously, my mind is going to bend in on itself

Knows Osama Bin Laden would still be alive if he hadn't crawled out of his cave to take advantage of Pizza Hut's NEW Ultimate Cheese Lover's™ pizza special. Fuck the world.

Let's hope no media organizations confuse "Osama" with "Obama"

I have no desire to cheer for death when there is so much that perpetuates immediate, nearby, and global violence every day.

WTF for real? So that means we can have our military back now, yeah?

Any way we can get his body on the space shuttle before it takes off, you know eject him into the cosmos

Remembrance of the beautiful souls we've lost along the way

How about we just shut our TVs off and have a meal together? Wouldn't that feel good?

I thought Chuck Norris killed Osama before he was even born

Does not celebrate anyone's death. Sorry.

That's good news about Osama, although I'll definitely miss his hilarious Twitter feed.

"But I'm watchin' Cupcake Wars, Laura!" —GW Bush

Eight-year anniversary of "Mission Accomplished."

What shameful gloating.

"America this is quite serious. / America this is the impression I get from looking in the television set. / America is this correct?"

Wait Osama wasn't in Iraq?

How bout we auction the body at Sothebys and use that money to pay down the debt?

Can't help but think that one person's death doesn't really solve anything.

Y'alls are brainwashed America can't go 5 seconds without ketchup everywhere

The pledge of allegiance was a nice touch. but WWFS? (What would Foucault say?)

Patriotism is tacky

"no body pushes me around i have heard / them say   land of the free they sing   what do / they fear mistrust betray more than the freedom /

they boast of in their ignorant pride   have seen / the squalid ghettoes in their violent cities / paradox on paradox   how have the americans / managed to survive"

America!!!!!!!!!!!!!!!! FUCK YEAH!!!!!!!!!!!!!!!

I'm neither happy nor sad nor relieved. My neighbors are setting off fireworks.

Smell you later, Osama.

How sweet would it be if Obama held up Bin Laden's severed head at the press conference

Rare to get to see a murder that makes the world such a better place.

I leave my computer for 1 hour and Osama bin Laden is suddenly dead?!

"Even gluing stones to garbage"

won't save the world
even putting a purple film filter
over the firmament
won't save the world
sandbags and unlit grids
and volunteerism
won't save the world

we are already fucked
and waiting
eyes on the slow demise
that will reach us
after we are dead
like the signal from a star
a hundred light years away

what I wanna know is
when we kill the earth
and the earth kills us back
who will keep their eyes
on the moon

If the world didn't end on December 21, 2012

then we drove twenty
　　　　　out of twenty-four hours
　　　　crossed every state
　　　stalled for hours in Ohio snow
　　　　in a snake of red brake lights
while the world decided to halt or inch along
　　　　　never learning what was up ahead
　　glad to be breathing
　　　　　　exhausted and pushing on
　　toward bad directions in Indiana
　　　　　hurling us off onto country roads
　　toward a diorama
　　　　of small-town America past
then giant windmills for miles
　　　　　nightlights pulsing in unison
flew us to the moon
　　　I was your Sancho insisting
　　　　　　　carry on
　　　　we are fools
　　　　　　　carry on
　　the kosmos is tilting and
　　　　the cats are howling in the back
　　and at four in the morning we arrived
　　　　　at the house where I grew up
which had gotten so far away
　　　　so completely of a different era
　　that I was no longer coming home

Open Season

I get all my news from the weather report or
I get all my weather from my news feed or
windows refuse to tell me what I wanna know.
Beat cops & Freedom Tower & Mobil sign

& "Zero Viz," the song that gets the last
laugh. Ha, ho, oh, I'm gonna get curtains one
of these storms & I am going to get down
from here one of these days. The season

between Sandy & Nemo, three months of
sandbagged nesting & now we use hot breath
& the flats of our fists to make animal tracks.
We weren't bombed out, we were bombed in.

Calling all groundhogs, calling all perennials,
all you strange herds & goodhearts, come on.

Diamonds (Dash Cam Remix)

I went to see what that flash in the sky was about
and then the window glass shattered,
    bouncing back on me.
My beard was cut open, but not deep.
They patched me up.
              It's OK now.
After the flash, nothing happened
    for about three minutes.
Then we rushed outdoors.
       I was not alone,
       I was there with Katya.
The door was made of glass,
    a shock wave made it hit us.
I opened the window from surprise—
      there was such heat coming in,
as if it were summer in the yard,
and then I watched as the flash flew by
      and turned into a dot
        somewhere over the forest.
I saw a flash in the window, turned toward it
   and saw a burning cloud,
     which was surrounded by smoke
     and was going downward.
Then the light went out
    and the trail began to change.
The changes were taking place within it,
    like in the clouds,
         because of the wind.
   I saw a light,

it looked like it was from a nuclear explosion,
       like I had seen in documentaries.
    It was a light which never happens in life,
it happens probably only in the end of the world.
       I am at home, whole and alive.
I have gathered together my documents and clothes.
    And a carrier for the cats.

[February 15, 2013]

Derailed

with Former Congressman Patrick Murphy @USAMurphy

Glad you are okay. Looking to see if Fox News and affiliates can get permission to use your picture.

CBS News here can we have permission to use this photo? we will credit, Hope all are okay!

glad you're ok & helping Mr. Murphy. May 6abc/WPVI-TV & its licensees use your photos without limitation in all media?

Glad you're OK. Do you mind if United Press International uses your photos across all platforms with credit? Thanks.

yo pat this picture is rad as fuck this is ron over at buzzfeed please add me on instagram if I can profit from ur pain

hello can CBS Boston use your photos of the train accident with a courtesy?

Hey Patrick, hope you're ok. I was wondering if I could use this picture for the cover of my debut album.

glad you're okay. . . @cbschicago and affiliates asking if we have permission to use your photos.

Hi Patrick, I work at WBAL in Baltimore. Do we have permission to use your photo?

Glad you're okay, Patrick. can i print this picture onto a cake for my son's birthday?

Can we get your permission to publish this photo in tomorrow's Philadelphia Inquirer?

When you have time: Would you be willing to let @latimes use this photo? Best wishes.

Sounds like an ordeal, I hope everyone's Ok! Do you mind if I get a giant tattoo of this pic on my back? Will give credit.

Can the Daily Mail Online run your image in our coverage? Please let us know.

Glad your okay, but more importantly, can I have permission to use your photo for my nephew's Bar Mitzvah?

Hi Patrick, best wishes to you and the other passengers. May I use this as my yearbook photo? I'm graduating

May PIX11 News use your photos?

My goodness. Prayers for all. Do I have your permission to shave this image into the back of my head?

glad you are safe and helping others. Can NY1 use you photo with courtesy?

can I use it on my Christmas card this year? Fav for yes

prayers to everyone involved. Can I use this image to test out my new 3D printer? With permission, of course.

pat if you don't respond in the next 5 minutes with the name of your favorite dave matthews band song you forfeit photo

Glad to hear you're okay. Can we use your photos on @CBSNewYork?

Can we have permiss. to use ur pic as a metaphor for @HillaryClinton's handling of #Benghazi?

Such an ordeal! I have used this image on a series of commemorative plates.

Happy Birthday USA

Try pairing gluten-free crackers
with a large picture window
    your morning au lait
            with a refreshed radar
on weather dot com
    Stormwatcher's Delight is a little like
            Stoner's Delite
    You've got your sweet you've got your salt
your concessions and your frame
            Now let it melt—
Arthur, once magnanimous, now
    demoted to four-eyed aardvark
            "The populace was aghast to learn
                more people die in hurricanes
                named after cartoon characters"
    And many, too, are conceived
in apocalyptic log cabin fever
            mistaken for lust
If we're fucked then fuck us till it's over
            The world ends
                in a flare of proliferation
    Blueblack steels the sunset
            The stadiums all empty
a spawning—and then—a dawning

Telewitness

I blew up a bed
by the TV
and slept

the afternoon away—
not a bomb
an air mattress

I blew up a bed by the TV
and listened for explosives
I was far from the danger

I was an official telewitness—
on the screen no one had slept
no one was American anymore

what right did they have
the threat was out there
the threat was in here

the threat
thumped inside
my chest

shelter in place
tender classmates
we can see you

with our thermal camera
we can see
his death wish

the bloody botch
the half-life of the tweet
the ways these things go

"Safe to call this the first
crowdsourced
manhunt?"

he was the bomb
vs.
the bomber

I won't divide the world
into those who find the links
and those who sever them

because you see
how I'd be guilty
either way

we have words and
touch and what look like
different bodies

we are knowable
by our skin
scraped and punctured

it's a miracle
we stay separate
and unharmed

it was we
who made all these
sharp-edged things

but have no
armor
most of us

shake a hand
say thank you
say happy birthday

it's a miracle these
Saturdays of honey-
light parties

and no one bloody
on the floor

precarious

not like walking
on a tightrope

but like walking
to the mailbox

I was far from the danger

I rarely feel safe
or almost always
am

"I guess it's too late to live on the farm"

It's never too late to live on the farm though the crops
may have rotated
beyond recognition. It's always too late to move to the farm
but it is good to cultivate longing.
I guess.
The farm inspires in me a fecund moralizing. Land lets
the cityslick feel
a longing for the past, then a hardscrabble farewell.
Who is there to talk to
on the farm, and do we accept a vague lowing.
Can the ultracontemporary
ever be rural? Probably not. I need the farm to remind me
this spotty dailiness
was chosen. By me. I always moved to my farms
whenever their specters pulsed
and now I am very tired. . . .
The farm, always arriving, mottles whatever's at hand.

Liberty in the Basement Light

The portal pukes me out

I roll and roll I'm breaded with gravel.

Get up dust myself off and in all the sidewalk planters, mannequins with my old outfits on, tableaux of my phases.

Say a little prayer of my heart's desire, Mom said.

Bare knees in the cement.

I got to the other side. Not another movie set but the only place I'd ever wanted that way—moist lipped, open armed, no nostalgias clanging around in my satchel like antique tins. I didn't miss them.

I kneel past the end of the prayer and into the sting. The city's in my blood and my blood's sloshed on the stone. I'll build a world this time.

I Pause and Look out over Brooklyn

Having traded a room of my own for a room with a view,
porch for fire escape, church for museum, lake for bays,
having swapped width for height, oak for elm, *elotes* for ices,
having passed through Nowhere, Indiana,
the clouds of Ohio pulsing with asymmetrical haircuts,
the wilds of Pennsylvania warning,
Jersey's great slide toward the sea,
having gotten the joke at the director's Q&A
and from every sidewalk angle heard two hundred guitars warbling,
having lost my way in the park and followed the glowing cherries back,
having answered all the cat's questions and all my love's entreaties,
having stuffed and built and hung,
taken the stairs down six flights and the elevator back up,
I pause and look out over Brooklyn.

What Am I Doing Here

tracking packages, moon phases
crooked streets that end at the sea

west was where the water was
now it's on all sides

you can tell by the slant of the sky
you can tell by the oil-slick indigo

city on a foam hill
girl sticking her limbs out the escape

planes fly upside down along
the decorative mirror

holding fancy sample perfumes and
shoes too nice to wear

don't know when to pay
or where to meet deliveries

don't know why the horizon
lights up at night

Poem

Rain makes New York
Old York

so we pose for a sepia
postcard

hot dog steam, Bergdorf Goodman
umbrellas and Prada

"as the enormous air of the avenue
lay pierced by rain"

I do this
I do that

turn the corner and see Bernadette
on an Acconci reel

walk in front of Nam June Paik's
projector

my silhouette briefly the star of
Zen for Film

conceptual art
in a selfie world

as a nod to poet security guards
everywhere

wear my Silver Jews T-shirt
to the steakhouse

where the captains nod and hum
"Very good, sir"

late night on Brevoort Place
the drops again

begin to blow
in the streetlamp's cone

Frank O'Hara by Alice Neel

Startled
as if he'd just heard news
from the lilacs

Or a child
chair-rigid
in a class portrait

New York School grad
yearbook quotes in memory
of his feelings

"you are of me,
that's what"
(1960)

Across from Clark Street Station

Sun comes out   rain comes down
   crowd huddled under awning
   stringèd swell of 30s soundtrack
shower scatters   umbrellas bob away

   I think of Whitman   of Crane
of Anderson (Wes)   even of Pound
   First flash flood of male influence?—
31   September   Brooklyn Heights

It's the light & the smell & the sound
      I think they'd like
graybeard   diver   dioramist   fascist
      lovers of the moving image

rise from the seats beside me   squabble
   beneath the awning   & scatter

Everything Changed in a Flash

Sudden Downpour On Brooklyn Bridge
Sudden Bridge On Downpour Brooklyn
Brooklyn Sudden Downpour On Bridge
Bridge Sudden On Brooklyn Downpour
Bridge Downpour On Brooklyn Sudden
Downpour On Brooklyn Sudden Bridge
Brooklyn Sudden Bridge Downpour On
Brooklyn On Sudden Downpour Bridge
Brooklyn Downpour On Sudden Bridge
On Downpour Brooklyn Sudden Bridge
Downpour On Bridge Brooklyn Sudden
On Sudden Downpour Bridge Brooklyn
On Bridge Sudden Brooklyn Downpour
Brooklyn Sudden Bridge On Downpour
On Downpour Bridge Sudden Brooklyn
Bridge On Downpour Sudden Brooklyn
Brooklyn Sudden On Downpour Bridge
On Bridge Downpour Brooklyn Sudden
Bridge Sudden Downpour Brooklyn On
Bridge Brooklyn Downpour On Sudden
Downpour On Sudden Bridge Brooklyn
Sudden Bridge On Brooklyn Downpour
Sudden Brooklyn Downpour On Bridge
Sudden On Downpour Brooklyn Bridge
On Sudden Downpour Brooklyn Bridge
Bridge Brooklyn Sudden Downpour On
Sudden On Bridge Brooklyn Downpour
On Brooklyn Downpour Sudden Bridge
Downpour Brooklyn Bridge Sudden On

On Brooklyn Bridge Sudden Downpour
Bridge Sudden On Downpour Brooklyn
Bridge Brooklyn On Downpour Sudden
Downpour Bridge On Brooklyn Sudden
Downpour Sudden Brooklyn On Bridge
Bridge Downpour Sudden On Brooklyn
Bridge Brooklyn Downpour Sudden On
Bridge Downpour Brooklyn On Sudden
Bridge On Brooklyn Downpour Sudden
On Bridge Sudden Downpour Brooklyn
On Downpour Bridge Brooklyn Sudden
Don't Forget How It Feels To Be Young

New York Bay

You asked
to be close
to weather

is this the shade
you requested
ma'am

fat flakes
asteroid crumbs
become

here on the prow
in gusts
they part for you

Saturday in the Park

I wasn't there
but I saw them lining up at the gardens
patient to hedge

the park got my friend drunk
my place a yielding couch at the edge
unbummy   safer, warmer
but with the same sundown ache

pollen sifts through screens & jesus
one of last night's ghost stories
jingling dogwood snow
or Xmas lights

well, sirs, aren't you aflutter
born again & again & again into the present
heathen in cement-bound heath

What Is Watching

two mirrors, one cracked
   birds too high to tell
that man couple, Bigses Lebowski
   the yellow-capped one's
over-the-shoulder
   "goddamn pigs"
and the plants that don't know
   who'll feed them or
what's a who
   the troll in the vent's
vigilant over still life
   can smell a quiver
/ / the virtue of Uncreatedness
   is pleasure in surprise / /
what might grow
   or follow a sidewalk
density of space over time
   if you can take the pressure
do, do

Port Authority

Say it ten times fast
and you're in purgatory.
JUDGMENT DAY
IS COMING MAY 21, 2011
"The Bible Guarantees It"
as does George Zimmer
Georg Simmel says
For, to be a stranger
is naturally
a very positive relation;
it is a specific form
of interaction.
"You Don't Need A PhD
To Read This Label"
boasts the drink
without taurine
that looks like a Big Gulp
so I take one.
You can't seem to graduate
from limbo
but the texts are manifold
and trifold
and you get to try out
your Jesus smile
when you say
No, thanks

How You Get Back In

To burrow back into the New Quotidian
we dream the tourist's nightmare

Pennsylvania whiteout, guardrails, black drop, one a.m.
missing rental car, Navy Yard impound, Jersey City mall

Reenter through World Trade mouth
surprised to find the drilling's so close & loud

We pick the steep bank's middle escalator
rise like steam from a sore

On the sidewalk I take a picture
mime a fanny pack adjustment

pretend I don't live here
where I've always wanted to live

The New York Miracle

in spite of all

that stops you

in your tracks

you trudge along

Your Big Sky

Underground for the count

        then up where the sky

    huge as promised

fills its bowl

          soupy grey

Fields & marshes

        dubious

            papier-mâché

The island always

above or below or behind

somewhere in there
      anything in the world

or out of it—

writing an homage to E. Equi

    disappointed to report
    no graffito asking
    "SKEETER, WHY?"
    any longer
    just my own

lurid scrawl
running the torch
along the track

on this dank day
scalloped & scholared

from California
to the New York Island

this sky is your sky, too

My Twentieth Century

You whizz by
space, time, speed
enchant us
me 'n' Mina
me 'n' Alice's Grandpa Bill
local made relative
your little magazines
pile up in the street
at the movies, on the moon
where we bring our baedeker
and we spell it wrong
we have fucked all the Futurists
every day in every way
I miss you, twentieth century
I remember you
with the fondness
of a native daughter
one hundred years ago
Monroe invented *Poetry*
and the *Titanic* sank
a plane into a skyscraper
and the New comes
crumbling down
I've being watching the
'Freedom Tower' go up
Falling towers
Jerusalem Athens Alexandria
Vienna London
Unreal

from my Brooklyn
'bedroom window'
The twentieth century
Frank was ashamed
was so entertaining
What fun
what fun we had
it has really been quite
a spectacle
Just free, that's all,
never argue with the movies
The twentieth century
at sea level how could we
ever make anything
new again
but I've stuck around this long
because I heart art

Decade Zero

A DECADE of zeroes
but we never gave it a name.
        We swiveled
    our necks
back toward the 90s
        shot-reverse-shot
and sometimes that meant more
        than a century ago
flower in buttonhole
        and so many stars seeable
some of them already dead.
            We ought ought *ought*
to look forward
        we admitted,
        barrette-snapping
carnations into green hair.
We grew gangly, sullen
        and wise
packing our lunchboxes
        for the future.

WITHIN ten years
all our favorite bands
    came out of hiding
reunited onstage
    in flannel
and rough wet
        hermit skin.
We'd been glistening
    all these years.
Anthems that'd known
    all the living rooms
in all the college towns
    we'd ever broken
    a lease in
sounded watery, tinny
    out of doors.
We held cans on strings
    up to our ears
to siphon each other's
        memories
    to hear a hole
being punched
    through the plaster
        of a room
that would never
        text us back.

It wasn't nostalgia
    or if it was,
      we won.
We didn't just wear bunny ears
and stand on a hill awaiting the signal.
      We got it back.

AT THE Y2K PARTY
 we shouted
Two! One! Zero! Zero! Zero!
  but time went on
and we trudged home and
laid our giant plastic
  2000 glasses
  by the bedside
When disaster arrived after all
   —one two, one two
and through and through—
  we stayed in our time zones
except those who traveled
  out of time
Orange with alertness
we stared at the red, boxy
   faces of clocks
carried few liquids
  stayed on the ground

WE WERE TRYING to remember
    what a hero was like
We remembered Ethan Hawke
    in *Reality Bites*
someone lazy,
      principled, pinko
last of the postwar
  whatever-I-damn-well-
    pleasers.
Now our heroes have to care
    even *less* than that,
we announced.
What's required
  is a self-reflexive leap
    past irony
      toward near-divine
      alienation!
And with that
we fainted into a heap
    from which we noted,
thinking of other dramedies
with great soundtracks:
    Better if the hero is a girl,
      and better if the word
    doesn't sound like a drug.

WE CROSSED the vast exurban plain
We went to the big box down the lane
    It was general
There were provisions available
We went to the big box for to find us a pony
       We could no longer see anything
      we weren't looking for
Every day in every way
      We went to the general store

Food slowed down, grew whole
        or stayed raw
        and we never ever
meant to slurp the ice off Kilimanjaro
it's just that we didn't know
        any farmers
even though some of us
        were from a place
for which the imagination
        suggested cows
    We were broke for years
    no supermarket to walk to
                    On the stardust trail
            LA, Chicago, New York
        we hardly knew ye
though you took all our money
and flashed your skyline grin
        against the mountains
rising from the frozen lake
    Gap-toothed you offered us your
plenty is never enough

WE THOUGHT back to
        unstructured time
You saw the loss of it like
        a hole in a steak
        stuffed with garlic
your drool dribbled into
        my schedule cleared
for the afternoon
        ignored the piles
on the floor
        watched a show
about the West
        If we held time
in our hands
        it was supple
& willing to give
        if we used
        shrink-wrap
& could keep it tender

I GO OUT to greet the pink sky
  is it petalful
  or chemical
past point of no return
or perfect three minutes
  I write this poem
  I do not
go out to greet the pink sky

We suggested
    Central Park or
    Empire State
but our mothers
always wanted to see
    Ground Zero
The rest of the year
    they sat worrying
        the warzone
"Hope no one you know
            was affected"
    as their heads
jerked along
            the ticker
Hi Mom,
  SoHo is a showroom
    Wall Street is
        a gated community
        The Hudson and
    East River flow
like capital
we are affected
    but can't point to
    a source
let alone make / do
    We are underused
    underemployed
    underimagined
we lack the slacker's

romance
and hardly even crave
or hear of it
anymore
here in the mourning
metropolis
of
lassitude

Hey nonny nonny
    We wandered round the town
Hey nonny nonny
    North & South upside down
Hey nonny nonny
    No GPS
Hey nonny nonny
    So depressed
Hey nonny nonny
    Directionless

WE RAN OUT of batteries
on an island in the bay
We were dead
We went back to the village
We didn't know how
to find anyone
We entered restaurants
without checking
star ratings
We walked into bars
a trio or a joke
Longer we'd wander
more we'd get charged up
We were trying to find
a place that meant
one hundred candles
but everyone kept saying it
in a bad accent
Then suddenly from a bar
with open windows
our friends leaned out
and touched our hands
We'd died and
gone back two decades
to learn of
a small world
To our inner compasses!
we toasted
shy and triumphant

all lit up
So we hadn't lost our old tricks
after all
eh
from when we were just thighs
wrapped in corduroy
We were just
magenta-haired things
feeling our ways
around town

VERY EARLY in the dark century
you said you would come
but you did not come

     very early

     dark

     a century

     a-rum-pum-pum-pum

WE FORGOT the words
   to the song
We think it went
   la la la la la
   don't you want me baby
It might have gone
   oh no baby don't go
We were playing
      decade trivia
   which wasn't a bar game
but an obsessive
      compulsion
   and the sky opened up
We were caught
   soggy and real
   whiteshirted
   protruding
It was a sign
   that we were where
we said we were
   and we were who
we said we were
   The words to the song
      didn't matter
there in the storm
   we were released
   we could move on
one foot in front of the other

not counting steps
some of us humming
very softly

RUINED CASTLES everywhere
             coming round
the Lincoln Tunnel helix
             sun zap
                prong rays
joke of panoramic vision
                privilege
                   we'd like to decline
are we responsible
                   for this vast ruined castle
how little can we care
                      and still be let in & out
at the gates
                Manhattan sunrise
                         should it contain
orange juice & tequila
                   or some other shot
unspoiled & uncontained
                straight to the heart

THE 90S WILL BE THE LAST NOSTALGIA
We have left the material world
The 90s will be the last nostalgia
Got my prints at the pharmacy
The 90s will be the last nostalgia
The insides were all smoky
The 90s will be the last nostalgia
The body, the marker, the knife
The 90s will be the last nostalgia
Bell-bottoms are back back back   back   back
The 90s will be the last nostalgia
I can see straight into their future
The 90s will be the last nostalgia
On a holiday from history
The 90s will be the last nostalgia
In the bathroom stall with my Discman
The 90s will be the last nostalgia
Show me your scars I'll show you mine
The 90s will be the last nostalgia
There's a light in your eyes that I used to see
The 90s will be the last nostalgia
Who you are and who you thought you'd be
The 90s will be the last nostalgia
Hard to remember what happened online
The 90s will be the last nostalgia
Can you miss what you can't touch
The 90s will be the last nostalgia
Get off an exit early, cruise the streets
The 90s will be the last nostalgia

The cops found me in the corporate forest
The 90s will be the last nostalgia
I don't believe that anybody feels the way I do
The 90s will be the last nostalgia
They found us in the warehouse
The 90s will be the last nostalgia
Time slow as a song
The 90s will be the last nostalgia
The sarcasm of the earnest
The 90s will be the last nostalgia
Don't let the daze go by
The 90s will be the last nostalgia
I'm not so lonely anymore
The 90s will be the last nostalgia
I'm never so lonely
The 90s will be the last nostalgia
Bright nook at the bookstore
The 90s will be the last nostalgia
Napster and shoplifting
The 90s will be the last nostalgia
Can't see the fiber optics
The 90s will be the last nostalgia
Couldn't see the lake
The 90s will be the last nostalgia
Could hear it roar
The 90s will be the last nostalgia
Make a wish, it counts thrice
The 90s will be the last nostalgia
Once for then, twice for now   now   now
The 90s will be the last nostalgia
I stroke your interface

The 90s will be the last nostalgia
        And it is not enough
The 90s will be the last nostalgia
        Will wonder survive
The 90s will be the last nostalgia
        When we have all the answers
The 90s will be the last nostalgia
        Like disco lemonade
The 90s will be the last nostalgia
        It's hard to get it right
The 90s will be the last nostalgia
        I'll just read it from my diary
The 90s will be the last nostalgia
        Are you a responsible recycler of images
The 90s will be the last nostalgia
        Put the best one at the start of the tape
The 90s will be the last nostalgia
        Rewind when you pass the house again
The 90s will be the last nostalgia
        Take me all the way
The 90s will be the last nostalgia
        Got a slacker time fetish
The 90s will be the last nostalgia
        Close the curtains
The 90s will be the last nostalgia
        We're done feeling that way

Popular Record

I Is Another

I is a product of this country
I is Made in the USA
I is "Born in the USA"
I is gonna be on TV one day
I has been practicing and
I is ready for her cameo
I is mediated but, like, saturated
I's screen is glossy hi-res
I dons the red white and blue
as a shawl and sings
Ding dong, the witch is dead
while skipping in a circle
I is too lavish to quit
I knows all the presidents
and all the state capitals
I knows she's a sucker even when
I walks among the rosebuds
I wants an untamed wildness but then
I feels like a French explorer
stockpiling beaver pelts and
discovering what's already found

More Lyrics for My Favorite Band

I was clapping for your dance / I was dancing for your clap

I was skooching around in my anger / fainting into a nap

and the girls on the train with their Warhol tote bags
and the girls on the train with their space! gusts
and the girls on the train empire-wasted
and the girls on the train shitfaced-ed!

I was scowling for your benefit / I was benefiting from your scowl

I was facepainting by number / hardsetting my jowl

and the girls on the train go

doo-da-doo / doo-doo da-doo

doo-da-doo / doo-doo da-doo

On the night before TV goes digital

PBS is playing *Chattanooga Choo-Choo*

ABC is playing the NBA finals (Los Angeles v. Orlando)

On NBC, the greenish light of a hospital room

CBS follows a tan blonde smirky genius

FOX's local news is sponsoring a conversion box giveaway

I am playing a dirge for my friend and tomorrow morning's
charges and tomorrow morning's pleading

Frasier reruns, *Cosby* reruns, cell phones spandex and storms

You say this is trivial but I take the long view

*that was the language we were hearing all night, the poetry of this
tall blond guy who spoke like the movies, stopping and starting,
making a joke, a kiss*

The poetry of television done up in Spanglish and white suits

This is a commercial-free hour

Baseball announcers play themselves

I play myself and Pavement's cover of "The Killing Moon"

Charlie Sheen and his patina

It's April in June, I've got bullion and butter as consolation

Little green flecks float to the surface

My instant / soup and its patina

What can I tell you that will exploit myself and no one else

The man with the red Indian on his cap has won the girl

Oh it's Charlie

Mennnnnnnn

The way to the surface is slow

Morbid, I'm leaving it on all night

[June 12, 2009]

Discontinued Motion Picture Products

Color Positive Film
Color Negative Film
B&W Positive and Negative Film
Intermediate Film
Sound Recording Film
High Contrast Panchromatic Films
Chemicals (Japan only)

[March 2013]

Leo as Gatsby

It was inevitable. Much wished for.
Our purest starhearts on the mark.
And so when the rest of the movie
was ludiglitz, we were all
Who cares, this is a *vehicle*. It drove us
wild to see him turn around at the party,
glass in hand. Three swoons for Romeo.
Juliet off someplace, fighting terrorism
and moods. Laureled but not emptied
enough to earn an American crown.
Jenny said he was a theater nerd
at poker games—bad fashion, not suave.
So he's, like, a really good actor?
Stuff him with money and let him die.
James Gatz   in the Ziegfeld
with our diamond headpieces
and 3D glasses. On the lobby sofa.
The casting couch. We came, we saw,
we crossed our legs. Some of us new money,
some of us royalty, some of us double,
some of us empty. None of us telling
the difference. A car, a bottle.
A room and an ice pick.
Bridges futurewashed with song.
The pool, the body, the light and the sound.
That summer when everything went wrong.

The Day Farrah Died

Went around all day
Trying to latch tears
Onto reason tried out
Twenty sentences to
Explain my rage my
Self-pity but none
Echoed just right
Only made me more
Friendless and sorry
Than was true and too
Interested in pointing
Still I blamed the sky
The pill the heat what
Ever came close but
Nothing could explain
These boulevard stretches
Those bangs nothing could
Explain a summer with
One less superheroine
One girl looping back
To an ancient sadness
Given up years before
Learn to say woman, learn
And now Michael Jackson
Too

B®AND LOYALTY

I was like so ... Geico

And you were like so ... Activia

And together we were like so ... GlaxoSmithKline

In an effort to be so ... Ann Taylor Loft

We end up so ... Crocs

And sometimes we're all like so ... Ambien

When we mean to be so ... Lemon Pledge Aerosol Spray

Although we're perfectly fine being Pilot G2 Retractable

We'd much prefer to be Crayola Classic Washable

Some days, we must accept, will just be Glad Press'n Seal Plastic Wrap days

I was Kotex Maxi Pads with Leak Lock Medium Flow with reluctance, but still I was Kotex Maxi Pads with Leak Lock Medium Flow

Even though you expected things to turn out so Comcast Triple Play

There's a communal relief to being so Verizon Wireless Nationwide Unlimited

In the end I'd just like people to remember me as being as iRobot Roomba 570 as possible

BOGO

fall back on some pioneering
sticktoitiveness

browse the big box
for DIY utopia kits

buy one get one
but I dunno

anybody
who likes getting lost in the woods

once you have been west and know
the west is not worth dying for

grind down your heels
in the here-now available dirt

No Slake

anchorless yearning
smelled like teen spirit
actually just shoplust

wandering around
the bodega looking
for something to buy

potatoes
in your dollar menu
apple pie

MSG molar clench
and all
american longing

starved for
to-be-invented
tastes

no one's offering so
let's try announcing
what we want

I go hungry
hungry
hungry

Shopping for Images

inside a dark greenhouse
inside a pharmacy
inside the mall
inside my mind

a girl beside
a hanging plant
reaches up
to touch a leaf

"my grandfather
told me
this was here
when he used to come here"

but only new dead things
fill the drugstore
and they're priced
to move

nostalgia as a product
in global modernity
there's a place for it
on the shelf

things take root
and keep growing anyway
what we miss
and how we keep

finding ways
to buy it back
deep inside the
deep inside

Insurgent Country

Freeway billboard children
stick antenna tongues out

Air's poised
sound on grass

What praise? sang the
microphone headset

Pious ashen depots—
their ache in tune

to somelips' want
for giant camera rolling

Drunken hills, child actors
dead marbles

and brownbagged
privacy of home-script

America so vast and
usable

popular record

( )

the moon is keeping the sun on
supermoon so huge and close
and tomorrow is spring
and daylight savings and march madness

( )

every once in a while I make a popular record
I like to keep it thinky but I like the real world too
so every once in a while I make a popular record
a record of the populous

( )

seems impossible the angle of light
will ever change or dim
I have a hunch
the moon is keeping the sun on

( )

Revolutionary Letters

A Knock at the Door

What can I come home to tell you
Now that I've code-broken
And stolen crib sheets for four cities
Just to be swollen with this waning empire wave
Just 'cause I knew a smallness and a smallness would not stick
What floats away floats away
Like a synthetic feather
Like most woman-and-child-made things
Enough to trick the flitting eye
But for the long gazer
Drifts a little shy
A little robotic down the breeze
I've come to tell you there won't be a knock at the door
So put down your sharp-edged letter openers
I've come to tell you if we're all being watched anyway
Then there will be a record of this
In a vault built from the granite wreckage of
ALL NEW RENO
From which far off they will extract the specimen
Smile!   like you might for a future
That won't know you or your kind—

A the Beaut

Here we go again, A—

time to lace your bonnet, buckle your galoshes,
glide with me headlong down the Slip'N Slide—

A, I sewed up the hole in my stretchy skirt just for you.

I needle-pricked my finger just for you ess ay

& we became bros.

.

.

.

Hand me the mic. I'd like a word with the rallying forces.

Read book Oprah toldja?

Check.

Can they sell that for you on eBay?

Double-check.

Seen kid-wishes pinned to balloon bouquets
drifting into the lighthouse's gaze over the lake in the fog?

Check again.

.

.

.

In spite of our averted eyes on the sidewalk

we are nightly flying door to door

as a fridge door glows, as an engine stalls

delivering all that's fit to print

of "what is found there"

Law of the Riot

The question of the existence of God has become a political question

Since 1845 in New York three or more people can't wear masks unless they're coming from a masquerade

In Russia they made the mask law in spring 2012

This is first of all an open civil conflict with an authoritarian regime

In Russia democracy is a newborn baby

It was idiotic choreography in my opinion

But it was not blasphemy

In a sense what was criminal was the intent

This is first of all an open civil conflict

But it was not blasphemy

Some of the words were offensive to the patriarch personally

But it was not blasphemy

They were hitting an invisible enemy with their fists

Democracy is a newborn baby

But it was not blasphemy

blasphemy

blasphemy

blasphemy

The Machine Does End

I say

to the tinny beeps

in the house

my friend is not here

nor do I have

any further information

and you may not train your spyglass

on my dreams

The Shock of the New

that art it
burned me
with frayed
prongs

don't
stick it in the socket
stick it in the socket
don't

lightning
one of nature's
number one
killers

aghast
I thought I'd die
of shame
at their unhinged

skulls
their feathered
mynxed
muffs

swinging
and sparking
in the armory
aisles

The revolution starts at home

The revolution will be ready in, like, half an hour
The revolution is shedding like crazy
The revolution thinks it's time to put the screens back in
The revolution wobbles at the corner
The revolution leans into the window to hear you clearly
The revolution has a room of its own
The revolution like a dust bunny blows from center to margin
The revolution left the bong packed for you
The revolution is staid and plaid
The revolution can't find the can opener
The revolution hates puns
The revolution should stop hitting refresh and get on with its day
The revolution thinks it's too old for icicle light strings
The revolution only does the dishes it needs
The revolution needs a proper spice rack
The revolution gets bunchy at the corners
The revolution has vowed to use its chin-up bar every morning
The revolution left its keys in the door
The revolution makes the cat jealous
The revolution knows way up here is a battlement
The revolution flags like basil leaves on the fire escape

Administered

The forceps pinched my nose
I chewed through
    the leather strap
    bolted up
went howling
    toward the emergency exit

Fire escape
caught my flight at the rail
    swaying above the city
    gazing down on
what looked less like ants than
    capsules
in a quarter machine

Maybe I saw the light
    maybe not
as I went sliding down the rail
    sure of my musculature
    sure of my skeletor secret

My body escapes administration
    because of lack of decision
    because of dumb blonde luck—

If a decision not to make a decision
    is still a decision
then all I can tell you is how
    I didn't really *decide*

to shoot out the bottom of the escape
    a twenty-five-cent toy prize

to fall into step
  with the podded masses
    who by virtue of creeping
      between buildings
  and sliding down rails

  evade forceps and straps
      machines and laws
the claw that tries to grab
    your stuffed animal skull
and grips too late—

I walk the long halls

I walk the long halls maybe of my mind
But maybe of a city that's real
I walk the long halls, take a picture
Maybe in words
There is a door marked with a purple X
Is it for me?
There is a sky ferocious in its switch-ups
Hiding a beyond hiding a beyond
Time is a dimension
Does anyone remember?
It is no small thing
Is it for us?
I walk the long halls
Like elevators to the planets
I have a hard time imagining space
Without the rings in drawings
I walk the long halls
Which you can do even by sitting still
It is just the effort it takes to keep moving
Forward in time ⎯⎯⎯⎯⎯⎯⎯→
The long halls are made of light
And shadow and go in every direction
Even diagonal and backwards
The halls are like a three-dee
Word search
Which is like a poem
In the long halls I hope to meet you
Where you've fallen forward
And slide along. . . . .

"O victory forget your underwear we're free"

O victory you're teary and gassy

O victory they dumpster'd your books

O victory you find me out while I ride underground

O victory you came slowly and growly all across America

O victory you came and found me I did not try to win

O victory from Arab spring to deep wet fall

O victory there's no end to this, you jump on the wheel right where you are

O victory free already and where does freedom go

O victory I'm spinning (the skin I'm in)

O victory to the bridge to the park to the square to the streets

O victory if we could if we could touch

O victory tongues, tongues, tongues

O victory I'm falling for you they've got me by the tase

O victory from afar while I click and glow I see and know

O victory in the cries of the waterlogged librarians

O victory in the char of lowest Manhattan

O victory goes commando wears no underthing

Kept Busy

set my screens down
in a row like potions
for forgetting

an accidental empty hour
gapes
till I ask what I want

to be able to see stars
why's it so hard to touch grass
have I ever not lived in cities?

I have to stop and think
not like I don't know
my own story

but like I can't
remember
which part's dreams

finally resting by accident
hustle-howls   sunny sirens
sucked up into soundproof

eyes closed I dress
sidewalk scenes
with mossy smocks

accessorize
with something viney
twig-snappy

add a gurgling brook
a tree falls across
I hear it

empire wane

Look there
ye mighty

back on the beach
it's us

in our
hotpants

wriggling our way
out

Acknowledgments & Notes

Thanks to the editors of the following journals and anthologies, which published earlier versions of many of these poems: the *American Poetry Review*; the *Atlas Review*; *Columbia Poetry Review*; *Delirious Hem*; *electric pumas*; *Eleven Eleven*; *Esque*; *Everyday Genius*; *Fence*; *Finery*; *Ghost Proposal*; *glitterMOB*; *Horse Less Review*; *InDigest*; *Maggy*; *No, Dear*; *The Portable Boog Reader*; *Sink Review*; *Somnambulist Quarterly*; *Super Arrow*; *City of the Big Shoulders: An Anthology of Chicago Poetry*; *The Great Gatsby Anthology*; and *The &NOW Awards 3: The Best Innovative Writing*.

Some of these poems also appeared in the chapbooks *Nonstop Pop* (Bloof Books, 2013), *Merrily, Merrily* (Lame House Press, 2013), and *Seer / Sucka* (Dusie Books, 2011).

Thank you to everyone who read and commented on these poems, especially (G)IRL: Hanna Andrews, Marisa Crawford, MC Hyland, Lily Ladewig, Caolan Madden, and Jennifer Tamayo.

Thank you to Shanna Compton and the Bloof Books fam: I feel so lucky to have an editor and peers who are also my poetry heroes.

•

The title "**Everything's Been Recruited**" (9) comes from Caryl Churchill's play *Far Away*.

The title "**Under the terrible burden of destiny laughing as a young man laughs**" (13) is from Carl Sandburg's poem "Chicago."

The text of "**We Got Him**" (14) comes as-is from social media and contains lines from Allen Ginsberg's "America" and Robert Hayden's "American Journal," as they appeared on social media.

The title "**Even gluing stones to garbage**" (17) comes from Joyce Mansour's poem "Forgotten Hours of the Law," and the poem was written for the reading "Dolorous Bubbles Delirium: Celebrating Joyce Mansour" organized by Shanna Compton and held at Two Moon Café in Brooklyn on November 17, 2012.

Diamonds (Dash Cam Remix) (20) takes its text from testimonials following the Chelyabinsk meteor explosion and is meant to be read over Rihanna's song "Diamonds." (Listen at electricpumas.tumblr.com.)

The text of **Derailed** (22) comes as-is from social media.

"I guess it's too late to live on the farm" (30): The title comes from Bernadette Mayer's "Essay." Thanks to Natalie Eilbert for the prompt; you can read the other responses on the *Atlas Review*'s website.

The section title **Liberty in the Basement Light (31)** is from Cat Power's song "Manhattan."

In **Poem (36)**, the line "as the enormous air of the avenue lay pierced by rain" is from Frank O'Hara's poem "Homage to André Gide."

In *Frank O'Hara* by **Alice Neel (38)**, the line "you are of me, that's what" is from O'Hara's "Cornkind."

Everything Changed in a Flash (40) uses Brion Gysin's permutation method.

What Is Watching (44) borrows from Alice Notley's poem "The Virtue of Uncreatedness."

The italicized lines in **Port Authority (45)** quotes "The Stranger" by Georg Simmel, trans. by Kurt H. Wolff.

Your Big Sky (48) is for David Trinidad, who introduced me to the New York School. The phrases "SKEETER, WHY?" and "lurid scrawl" are from Elaine Equi's poem "Trenton Local."

My Twentieth Century (50) is for my PhD-qualifying exam committee: Harriet Davidson, Elin Diamond, Evie Shockley, and Cheryl Wall. "Falling towers . . ." is from T.S. Eliot's "The Waste Land." "Just free, that's all, never argue with the movies" is from O'Hara's "Fantasy."

At the Y2K Party (58): "one two, one two / and through and through" is taken, with modified punctuation, from Lewis Carroll's "Jabberwocky."

More Lyrics for My Favorite Band (80): My favorite band is Destroyer.

The italicized section of **On the night before TV goes digital (81)** comes from a blog post on *Harriet* by Eileen Myles about Steve Carey.

The title **Shopping for Images (89)** comes from Allen Ginsberg's "A Supermarket in California."

Insurgent Country (91) was inspired by the film *Jesus Camp*.

Law of the Riot (98): All text was transcribed (and sometimes repeated and reordered) from "Pussy Riot and Protest: The Future of Dissent in Putin's Russia and Beyond," a conversation with Pussy Riot's Russian attorneys, NYU Law School, September 21, 2012.

The title **"O victory forget your underwear we're free" (106)** is from Allen Ginsberg's "Howl."

Sorry, Shakespeare; thanks, tabloids.

About the Author

Becca Klaver is the author of the poetry collections *Empire Wasted* (Bloof Books, 2016) and *LA Liminal* (Kore Press, 2010) as well as several chapbooks. She was a founding editor of the feminist press Switchback Books and is coeditor of the multimedia poetry anthology *Electric Gurlesque* (Saturnalia Books, 2017). She attended the University of Southern California (BA), Columbia College Chicago (MFA), and Rutgers University (PhD), and in the spring of 2017 will be the Arts & Sciences Distinguished Visiting Writer at Bowling Green State University. She lives in Brooklyn, where she cohosts the podcast *The Real Housewives of Bohemia*.

Praise for *Empire Wasted*

Empire Wasted is an astonishing book, anthemic in its catchiness and the power of its arguments. From the suite of "Decade Zero," the years so vacant they don't even have a name, and the concomitant attraction of the very dreariest productions of the 90s, through to the neo-di Prima fervor of the revolutionary letters, it hits all the right notes. While this historical drift, this gathering political consciousness is one we see around here in the SF Bay Area every day, the difference in the NYC version is fascinating—especially with that Midwestern twist in the narrative—the Gatsby twist. Becca Klaver has written a book for her generation that manages, through its direct appeal, to speak to many older and younger than her years.

—Kevin Killian

Get out your Ozymandias hot pants and your Warhol tote bag: Becca Klaver is throwing a rooftop party for the end of the world. Everyone's there, scrolling through the Pentagon's Instagram feed and moshing to the sound of TV going digital. These poems whiplash through the last three decades, through the American landscape, through the songs stuck in your head, Klaver taking us from the last nostalgia to the New Quotidian. These are our anthems, bitches. Turn them up.

—MC Hyland

What is America? And what is New York City? Where are we in history, and how will these days, years and decades live on? With *Empire Wasted*, Becca Klaver asks these impossible-to-answer questions and more, taking us on a road trip across America and across the shaky threshold from the last century to the present one. Recalling Notley and Didion, Klaver gets "bad directions" that lead through a portal "to a small-town / diorama of America Past." In "At Night the States," Notley writes, "at night the states / I forget them or I wish I was there." In a decade in a century in a country when we were told to "never forget," Klaver remembers more than what she's instructed to. Like pictures in a shoebox or a Facebook album, she shuffles through memories and snapshots both personal and country-sized, looking for truth, looking for home, finding it nowhere and everywhere.

—Marisa Crawford

Becca Klaver's *Empire Wasted* is an ode to a forever evolving and surviving New York City. These poems waltz with nostalgia. Along with Klaver, we slouch back towards the 1990s. We get drunk in dark bars when all the electricity goes out. We count down to the year 2000. Dead cell phone in hand, Klaver celebrates the writers and revolutionaries who inhabited the city before her. The television has gone to static and we're out on the fire escape, the whole world heating up below our dangling feet.

—Lily Ladewig